FEARLESS

Farris Lind, the Man Behind the Skunk

by Rick Just

Other Idaho Books by Rick Just

Idaho Snapshots
Keeping Private Idaho (a novel)
100 Years, Idaho and Its Parks
Images of America, Idaho's State Parks
A Kid's Guide to Boise

Copyright © 2019 by Cedar Creek Press, LLC

ISBN 978-0-9986261-4-7

Published by Cedar Creek Press, LLC

Boise, Idaho

All rights reserved. No part of this book may be reproduced or transmitted in any form or by any means, electronic or mechanical, including photocopying, recording, or by any information storage and retrieval system, without written permission from Cedar Creek Press, LLC.

CONTENTS

1. **DAREDEVIL** 2
2. **THE GUY'S GOT GAS** 18
3. **FLYING FIGHTERS** 28
4. **I HATE BUGS!** 32
5. **A SKUNK IS BORN** 40
6. **SIGNS OF THE TIMES** 48
7. **TRAGEDY** 64
8. **FIGHTING THE FIRST LADY** 70
9. **CARRY ON** 74
10. **TRANSITIONS** 86
11. **SUNDRY SIGNS, ETC.** 90

ACKNOWLEDGEMENTS

My thanks to Stacey Smekofske and Gretchen Mullens for their editing skills and Jennifer Okerlund for her advice on design. For help with historical photos and permissions, thanks to Katherine Jones, Alisha Graefe, John Bertram, Aaron Esparza, and Nick Collias. Thanks to Mike Russell, director of operations for Stinker Stores for pointing me in the right direction more than once. Thanks, also, to Renee' Johnstone, marketing specialist for Stinker Stores, and current keeper of the skunk. This book would not be the same if it weren't for my opportunity to study the fine tribute Farris Lind's family wrote some years ago. Though not readily available to the public it was lovingly done and provided much insight into the man they fondly remember. Special thanks to Ed Harris for the sign photos that are such an integral part of this book. Ed's dad, Fred, worked for the Idaho Transportation Department for many years. As a little hobby, he took pictures of the Stinker Station signs whenever he saw one. Ed stressed that, "he always did it when he was off work."

Dedication

For J. Kent Just
who knew how to laugh

CHAPTER ONE

DAREDEVIL

Tarzan—The Twin Falls-Jerome Bridge was some 1500 feet long and about 475 feet high when it was built in 1927. Lind family lore has it that Farris Lind—not yet Fearless Farris—and a friend delighted in crossing the canyon through the gridwork beneath the bridge swinging from one steel brace to the next, dangling above the Snake River. The bridge was said to be the highest in the world at the time.

Farris Lind was a bit of a daredevil, a risk-taker, and a man with a propensity for plunging into things, sometimes with no plan and only a moment's contemplation. He was also generous, hard-working, inquisitive, ambitious, and self-assured. His sense of humor would one day make him famous.

Farris started exhibiting those qualities early on. Born in 1915, he grew up on the outskirts of Twin Falls, Idaho, in a struggling farm family. Young Lind saw no shame in being from a humble family. The kids went to school in the winter in a covered wagon with hot bricks bundled at their feet to keep warm. He could not help but envy the kids who showed up at school in a car, sans hot bricks at their feet.

Lind saw that hard work was the way to get ahead in life. So as a teenager, he took whatever odd jobs came along. He thinned a lot of beets as a kid.

He once took a job to earn money to go to a high school dance, illustrating his penchant for hard work. It was during the Great Depression, about 1933 or '34, that he and a friend, Blaine Taylor, took on the task. They shoveled 40 tons of coal out of a train car and onto a conveyor belt. They did it in one, long, hard, sweaty day. It earned them $25 each, which would have made a nice pocket of change to spend on their dates. Ironically, the pair was so worn out and sore from shoveling coal that they had to pass on the dance (Family, Fearless Farris: The Incredible Life of a Courageous Man, 2005).

In high school, Lind hung out a lot at the Twin Falls airport pestering pilots for rides. When he was a senior, he took lessons. His interest in flying would serve him well in the impending war and later as a biplane-flying businessman.

Lind took his older brother Wyland up in a Piper Cub early on, demonstrating stalls and spins. After they landed, Wyland's stomach revolted. Farris later teased him saying, "[that he] was the only fellow I knew who could eat a roll for breakfast and vomit a seven-course meal."

Paying for flying lessons and the flying itself had Farris scrambling for money. He took manual labor jobs whenever he could get them. In 1934, when he was a senior, he landed a job in the movies. It was not a spectacular job. He was an usher at a Twin Falls theater. Soon he began filling in for the manager. It was in this movie house job that Farris first showed the talent that would set him apart.

Theaters at that time promoted the movies they showed with little or no help from the movie studios. Lind made up posters and distributed them around town, advertising upcoming shows. Farris had flair, and the theater manager turned all the promotion over to him.

When Lind graduated from high school, he knew college was not in the cards because of the expense. He took his talents in movie promotion to Salt Lake City and got a job as the assistant manager of Capitol Theater. The Capitol was part of the Intermountain Theaters chain. He wasn't there long before the company sent him back to Idaho to manage a pair of theaters, The Grand and the Isis, in Preston. He did well, sharply increasing attendance.

Living in Idaho turned out to be a temptation for Farris. He was sweet on a girl in Twin Falls. He longed to see her though he didn't have the time to spare due to running the theaters. That Twin Falls romance lured. Farris trained his ticket sellers and ushers to run the theaters so he could then slip away. He'd climb into his Model A and hit the road for Twin Falls, 150 miles away.

Things went perfectly with the self-managed theaters, until they didn't. The projection booth in the Isis caught fire during a showing while Lind was in Twin Falls. The fire department put it out without a great deal of damage to the theater. However, the young lady nominally in charge that night got flustered dealing with refunding money to patrons, figuring out how to clean things up, and what to do next. She called management in Salt Lake. Lind's game was up, and so was his

Movie Man—Farris Lind managed a couple of movie theaters in Preston for a while when he was just out of high school. He tried juggling his job with a long-distance romance, sneaking away from Preston to visit his girlfriend in Twin Falls while his employees showed movies. That scheme went up in flames when one of the theaters caught fire while he was out of town.

career in the movies.

That's when the letter came.

Farris Lind could be a little impulsive in his early days, which is why he fell for a scheme that we would recognize today as akin to getting an email from a Nigerian Prince. The racket was called getting a "Spanish prisoner letter." The letter Lind received was from a businessman who was in a Mexican jail for embezzling $250,000. Supposedly, the businessman had gotten young Farris Lind's address from a mutual acquaintance "who must not be named."

If Farris would only come to Mexico and bribe a certain prison guard with $500, the businessman would get claim checks out to him allowing Lind to pick up a trunk with a false bottom, beneath which he would find the $250,000. The businessman wasn't concerned about himself. He just wanted someone to take the money and get his 18-year-old daughter—no doubt a stunning beauty—out of Mexico and into the United States (Farris Lind... Flotsam on Gasoline Sea, 1959).

Lind borrowed the money against an insurance policy and headed for Mexico. He paid the guard $500 but found no trunk filled with loot. He then learned from a U.S. Consul officer that this was an old scheme many had fallen for, and there was no chance of getting his money back.

The trip back home in a third-class mail coach offered plenty of time for reflection.

Shortly after returning from Mexico, Farris got a job in the industry he would eventually upend in Idaho. He became a gas jockey at a cut-rate station on the edge of Twin Falls.

Over the years, many stories have been written claiming that Lind "owned his own station" at age 20. Not so, though the man who did own it left the running of the business mainly up to Lind.

Lind's first innovation at Woodlawn Gas was to tint the gasoline. Why did people care what color their gas was, and how would they know in the first place? They knew because the ten-gallon glass container on the top of each pump showed what they would put in their cars. People wanted their gas to be a rich amber color because they thought it was superior to clear gasoline. There may have been some truth to this. Independent stations, such as Woodlawn, got their product from small Wyoming refineries. It was clear, or near to it. The more expensive, higher octane gas sold by major oil company refineries was a nice amber. So, Farris tinted the clear gas at the station with dye (Family, Fearless Farris: The Incredible Life of a Courageous Man, Circa 2005).

The richer looking gas was a hit, especially when he promoted it for 16 cents a gallon on signs at both ends of Twin Falls. Major brand stations were charging about 22 cents.

This was during the Grapes of Wrath days when down and out "Okies" were streaming westward. Spotting a chance for bargain gas, they would fill up anything they had that would hold liquid.

Farris endeared himself to Okies in another way. They were short of cash, of course. The manager at the discount station was happy to trade a few gallons

Color it Amber—This photo of a Model A pickup was taken at the Hyde Park Stinker Station in Boise circa 2018. The antique gas pump is just for display these days. That glass container on top had a couple of purposes. First, the attendant would ask how many gallons you wanted, and pump that much gas into the container before transferring it to your car. Second, you could see just what you were getting. In the early days it was common to water down gasoline. People could also inspect the color of the liquid. Cheaper, lower octane, gasoline was clear. Better gasoline was bright amber in color. When 20-year-old Farris Lind managed a cut-rate station in Twin Falls, owned by someone else, he got the idea that tinting the low-grade gasoline would make it sell better. And, yes, it did. (Photo courtesy of Stinker Stores)

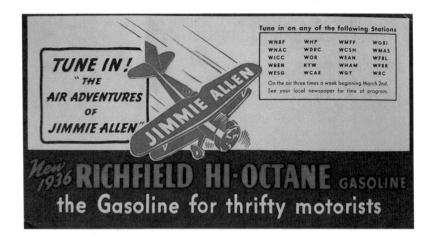

Radio Flyer—This 1936 advertising card for the radio program The Air Adventures of Jimmie Allen seems almost a foreshadowing of the life of Farris Lind. The fictional Allen had his adventures in a biplane, and the program was sponsored by a gasoline company. And here's the connection: Lind worked at an ad agency in Canada for a short time and answered fan letters for the program, signing them as "Jimmie Allen."

for whatever they had of value. He took in a lot of jewelry as well as guns and knives—anything they could get along without.

The job at the gas station lasted until a certain Cadillac entered Farris' life. His sister Arta and brother-in-law Spencer Grow came to Twin Falls in 1938 for a Thanksgiving visit, in a new Cadillac. The brother-in-law was in the radio business in Canada and was clearly doing well. Lind wanted to do well, too. He showed his brother-in-law the level of salesmanship he possessed by convincing Grow that he needed advertising help.

While in Toronto, Lind sold a lot of advertising and also found himself in charge of answering letters for fans of the popular "Air Adventures of Jimmy Allen" radio show. He would sign each letter as the fictional Jimmy Allen. After a few months, Farris and his brother-in-law had a falling out, and he returned to the U.S. (Farris Lind... Flotsam on Gasoline Sea, 1959).

Lind found a job in the oil business again, this time working in Denver for Conoco. There he met and married his wife, Virginia. Their romance and engagement lasted about as long as it took to write that sentence. Farris struck up a conversation with Ginny in a soda shop. He got her phone number and eventually worked up the courage to call and talk with her. They got to know each other a bit over the phone. Farris ended the conversation by asking her out. He picked her up for that first date at her parents' house. They went to a movie, stopped for a snack on the way home, and found themselves on the front porch. That's where and when Farris proposed. That impulsive proposition must have taken Ginny aback. She recovered though, and immediately accepted.

Shortly after, Farris and Ginny made a quick trip to Nebraska where there wasn't a cumbersome three-day waiting period and got married. They would be together for 44 years.

The newlyweds lived in Butte, Montana for a while. Then they moved back to Denver with Conoco. Farris, with a fledgling family to support, asked for a raise. None was forthcoming, so Farris and Ginny decided to try their luck in Lind's hometown of Twin Falls.

A Proposition—Virginia "Ginny" Lind in a 1961 Idaho Statesman *photo when she was Pi Beta Phi president in Boise. Farris met Ginny Johns at a soda fountain counter in Denver and asked her for her phone number. Later, he worked up the courage to call her. They chatted for quite a while before he asked her for a date. Farris picked her up at her parents' house and they went to a movie. After the film, they stopped for a snack, then went straight home. It must have come as a surprise to Ginny when Farris proposed to her on her porch that night. No less a surprise to Farris when she accepted. They eloped and were married November 5, 1939. They wed in Nebraska because that state did not have a three-day waiting period. They would be together for 44 years. (Photo courtesy of the* Idaho Statesman *and the Boise State University Library, Special Collections and Archive)*

CHAPTER TWO

THE GUY'S GOT GAS

Farris Lind was always alert to an opportunity. He and Ginny had been in Twin Falls just a few days in 1941 when an article in the paper caught his attention. It quoted Idaho's newly elected Governor Chase Clark as saying gasoline prices were too high. The governor had noticed that gas prices in other states weren't as high as they were in Idaho, and he encouraged the major petroleum retailers to give Idahoans a break. He even threatened to put the State of Idaho in the retail gasoline business, using a few pieces of surplus property (Farris Lind... Flotsam on Gasoline Sea, 1959).

Lind didn't know a thing about politics, but he understood how the big oil companies maneuvered to put independents out of business whenever they got a chance. He simply had to have a meeting with the governor.

Flat broke, he asked his younger sister Helen if she would loan him $5 so he could drive to Boise to get the governor's ear. She lent him the money, and Farris wasted no time. He headed out to Boise that very afternoon.

After he arrived in the capital city that evening, Farris slept in his Buick. The next morning, he washed up in a service station restroom, donned a coat and tie, and set out to meet the governor. Farris had no appointment. In a brash show of salesmanship, he talked his way past the governor's secretary and in a few minutes found himself shaking the hand of Chase Clark.

The 25-year-old with empty pockets had a tremendous gift of gab going for him. Governor Clark listened and became more and more convinced the brash young man knew what he was talking about. Lind said he could quickly bring the price of gasoline down in Boise if he could get a good deal on a place to operate. He knew the state had some scales on Front Street that were no longer in use. That spot would make an excellent place to put a cut-rate gas station.

Clark cautioned Lind that while he wanted to pressure the oil companies to bring down gas

Governor Gas—Governor Chase Clark, shown above pretending to be a potato farmer in a publicity photo, thought gas prices were too high in 1941. He publicly threatened to call a special session of the Idaho Legislature to give the state authority to either regulate the price of gas or enter the gasoline business. Farris Lind, a brash and broke 25-year-old with a keen eye for opportunity, talked the governor into leasing him a little piece of state land for a discount service station. He convinced Clark that it was the way to bring prices down in Boise.

prices, he also counted the men who controlled those companies as his friends and political contributors. He didn't want them pressured to the point where it would blow back on him.

The governor introduced Farris Lind to the state's attorney general, Bert Miller. Miller got the Farris pitch about the surplus scales on Front Street. The attorney general knew about the property, which officials had previously discussed without taking any action. To Lind's surprise and delight Miller agreed to lease the unused site to the pushy young man for $25 a month. Further, he agreed to defer payment of the first $25 until the second month of operation.

Such an arrangement today would take more time than a few minutes with the attorney general, and it would require much more paperwork. Idaho was still a lkind of cowboy in 1941, and deals were often done with a handshake.

Lind had met a man in Idaho Falls in the oil business who supplied much of the equipment needed to sell cut-rate gas, including a tank and a couple of pumps. He also fronted him his first load of fuel.

As things came together, Farris knew he'd need some operating capital. Remember that $5 his sister lent him? He'd asked his dad for a loan of $5 first and had been turned down. He went to his father again, this time asking for $2,000. Maybe pulling things together out of nothing impressed Herman Lind. Farris' father loaned him the cash. Farris paid it back on time and over the years gave many generous gifts to his parents from a new tractor for his dad to a new stove for his mom.

The property at the corner of 16th and Front Street in Boise was just right for that first station. Farris took out the scales, which left a nice pit into which he dropped a couple of 2,500-gallon tanks. He dumped gravel around the tanks and called that good. To say Lind cut some corners would be an understatement. There was already a small office on the site, complete with restroom, so he was quickly ready to go.

Cut-Rate—Farris Lind built his first cut-rate service station in Boise at the corner of 16th and Front, leasing a site where the State of Idaho had once operated a scale. The lower prices kept him hopping. On his first day in business, he pumped 2,000 gallons of gasoline. (Photo courtesy of the Idaho State Historical Society 1992-30-101-13)

Never one for subtlety, Lind advertised his product as "Governor Gas" for a while, going as far as pasting a picture of Chase Clark on his pumps. What the governor thought about the ploy is lost to history, but easy to guess. His face did not grace the pumps for long.

Governor or not, the station was a success from day one when Lind pumped 2,000 gallons of cut-rate gas. He had so many customers he barely had time to sleep.

If you wanted a paved lot, uniformed attendants, a free map, sparkling restrooms, and your tires checked, well, there were lots of major oil company stations in Boise where you could get all that. If all you wanted was cheap gas and oil from a likable guy who always had a smile, there was Farris Lind.

It was at that first location that Lind became Fearless Farris. A sign company approached him about putting up a neon sign. He liked the idea and worked out a deal where he could pay the sign off over a few months. It probably surprised the sign company that he didn't want the fancy sign on his leased property. He cut a deal with someone a couple of blocks down the street to have the sign installed there so it would attract people's attention in plenty of time to pull over for cheap gas. But what to put on the sign? Farris played the angle that he was the guy who wasn't afraid to take on the big oil companies. He had recently seen a movie featuring Al Capp's parody character of Dick Tracy, named Fearless Fosdick. Lind knew the alliteration would stick in people's minds. The Fearless Farris sign featured a man wearing boxing gloves and striking a fighting stance. The skunk would come later.

CHAPTER THREE

FLYING FIGHTERS

For Farris Lind, 1941 was a terrific year. Until December 7. Not long after the Japanese bombed Pearl Harbor, Lind signed up for the war effort. He took on a partner to manage the Boise gas station while he was away and left for a stint with the U.S. Navy.

Lind was already qualified to fly multi-engine aircraft, so making him a pilot trainer was natural. His duties began with training at a private airport in Yakima, Washington. There he learned to fly the WACO UP F-7, a 220 HP biplane. He ended up spending much of his service time at Naval Station Great Lakes, training recruits in carrier flight, including training them to escape a submerged aircraft. It was dangerous work, and Lind was good at it. So good, that he remained a pilot trainer for the duration of the war and never saw combat.

During the war years, two children were born to Farris and Ginny Lind, Randy in 1942, and Julie Ann in 1943. Ginny and the kids got to spend time with Farris at Great Lakes.

Meanwhile, back in Boise, the gas business wasn't doing so well. There was a little profit each month, but gas was under ration because of the war. A person could buy about 16 gallons per month, which didn't go very far with the average car getting about 13 miles per gallon. The manager of the Boise gas station wanted out. Eventually, Lind's older brother, Wyland, took over the operation until Farris could return.

Lind's discharge finally came in December 1945, and he headed back to Boise, Idaho. Fearless Farris was back in the gasoline business.

CHAPTER FOUR

I HATE BUGS!

The cut-rate station was booming, again, under Lind's management. That didn't offer much of a challenge anymore, so Farris tried something new: DDT. While in the Navy, Lind had seen how effective the chemical was at killing bugs. This was years before the detrimental environmental effects of DDT were known; the colorless, odorless, and tasteless poison was effective.

Farris bought a couple of surplus military trucks, mounted tanks on them, and rigged them up for spraying. His advertising for the new service, which he ran out of Twin Falls, was blunt: "I HATE BUGS!" The slogan captured the attention of dairymen and farmers, launching the Fearless Farris Insect Control Extermination Company off the ground.

Okay, not off the ground. This was strictly a drive-around-and-spray-bugs business at first. It wasn't long, though, before Farris was taking to the air.

A friend from the Navy had heard about the

pest control business. He called Farris and offered to sell him three Piper Cub airplanes for $2,500 each to use for spraying crops.

In the years after the war, many pilots had the idea of making a living through crop dusting. Some of them were in Idaho and already in the skies, but Farris Lind had an advantage over those men when it came to setting prices. He could get fuel at wholesale.

As it turned out, he could also get cut-rate airplanes. Farris was able to bend the ear of Senator Glenn Taylor who lined him up with some war surplus planes. Taylor was an entrepreneur himself and probably felt Lind was a kindred spirit. After serving one term in the U.S. Senate and failing to win reelection, Taylor invented and marketed a toupee called "The Taylor Topper," buying cheap ads in men's magazines all over the country. The "Toppers" were a success, and the company is still in business today.

Lind was also buying ads in the local paper for

his new crop-dusting service. He bought enough that the *Twin Falls Times-News* didn't mind giving him a little free publicity. The paper ran an article that said in part, "Farris Lind… recently discharged Navy flier, will operate an aerial dusting service for Magic Valley farmers this season. He will maintain headquarters in Twin Falls for his fleet of six new planes that have been ordered." They also ran a picture of the smiling young pilot (Navy Airman Charts Valley Crop Dusting, 1946).

Finding pilots to fly his planes wasn't difficult for Lind. He knew many of them from his days as a Navy trainer. The pilots coming out of the war were mostly young men, some with more skill than judgment. It did not escape the notice of pilots that people often pulled off the country roads to watch them swoop down over the fields. It was like a free air show.

Some of the young men couldn't resist showing off. Benny Buchanan was an excellent pilot, and he loved proving it. On June 3, 1946, Buchanan had quite an audience. Several cars were parked on the road outside of Eden near the alfalfa field he was spraying. He even attracted a Greyhound bus full of onlookers. Rather than making a low-level run over the field and looping around for another run, Buchanan did hammerhead or stall turns at the end of each run. In a hammerhead, a pilot heads straight up into the air until the plane stalls, then jerks the rudder to bring the plane around 180 degrees, straight down. The dramatic maneuver at the end of each run and the beginning of the next had the crowd entranced until Benny lost control and slammed into a canal. He might have drowned if the impact had not killed him.

Less than a week later another of Lind's pilots, Rudolph Klunt of Nampa, caught a wing on a turn and crashed into a field seven miles south of Twin Falls. He was not badly injured.

In 1948, a string of crashes culminated in the death of another crop-duster, Charles Gallaher, 39, of Coeur d'Alene. His plane nosed into the ground northwest of Jerome. Earl Allen, another Fearless Farris crop duster, crashed two planes in the same

10-day period as the Gallaher crash. He was not badly injured in either incident. Allen said he was "through with crop-dusting flights" after the second crash.

In three years, the pilots crashed seven of the company's 12 planes, and two pilots were dead.

By 1949 there were a lot of people getting into the crop-dusting business; legal expenses were mounting up. It was time to get out. Lind sold his fleet of airplanes to a company in California and closed up shop. He was done with crop dusting, but not with flying. He took a Staggerwing Beechcraft as partial payment for his fleet. The enclosed biplane became his personal conveyance.

Here Comes the Skunk—The first Stinker Station was at the corner of 16th and Front in Boise. This photo is said to be from a press release in 1956, but judging by the vintage of the cars it could also be a few years earlier. Notice you might win free cash and you could get a free souvenir sticker. The station was selling tires, which it did in the early 1950s for a time. A sign boasts of the finest restrooms. That was a point of pride with Farris Lind. Selling cut rate gas didn't mean the stations had to be dirty.

CHAPTER FIVE

A SKUNK IS BORN

It was time to focus attention on those cut-rate gas stations. His business model was always to offer gasoline at a lower price than the major brand filling stations. That irritated the folks running those operations, and one of them said it out loud. According to a book about Farris Lind written by his family, the president of the Petroleum Marketing Association said in a newspaper interview that Farris Lind was a "real stinker in the market."

Lind latched onto that word and turned it into an honorific. He called himself a stinker. Then he got the idea of drawing up a skunk logo. The first one was a fierce-looking boxing skunk. That didn't last long. He thought a loveable skunk would be better, a' la Walt Disney. Soon the skunk became the logo for the company. It was also a mascot, just like the big boys had: Sinclair's dinosaur and Shell's tiger. Farris did them one better. Sinclair would never have a real dinosaur mascot, but Stinker could have a skunk. He caught a skunk, had it descented, and named it Cleo. He kept it in a cage

Always a Fighter—Some of the earlier skunks were a bit more aggressive than today's version. This ad from the November 12, 1950 Idaho Statesman *tells the origin story of the Stinker Stations. Born to fight the big guys!*

at the station at 16th and Front, letting it out for walks and on special occasions. Note that "Cleo," or another skunk was called "Lucifer" at least once in a Stinker ad.

Although that first cut-rate station at 16th and Front in Boise was a slap-dash operation, Lind was more meticulous as he added additional stations to his company. He bought the latest equipment and made sure everything was clean and shiny, especially the restrooms. Cut-rate did not have to mean tacky, in his mind.

The original Boise station got an upgrade in 1953. To celebrate, Lind ran a "most beautiful skunk in the state" contest. No word if anyone brought in a skunk to compete.

Although the main business was in Boise, Lind kept a vestige of his old bug-killing service in Twin Falls for some time. None of his employees sprayed from airplanes, but the service still worked the local orchards and fields. It wasn't making a lot of money, but hanging onto that business allowed

Lind to increase his "float."

In the days before electronic banking, one could count on it taking a few days for a check to hit the bank. Having the Twin Falls operation gave Farris a little extra float because it took at least three days for any check he wrote on the Twin Falls account to find its way through the mail. Furthermore, it took banks about three days to process an out-of-town check. If he wrote a check on the weekend, he could count on at least five days before it cleared.

There was nothing illegal about taking advantage of float. It was a common business practice, and a few household check writers counted on the same thing.

The Stinker stations were cash businesses. Farris would often deposit $4,000-$5,000 in a night drop box. That wasn't all profit, of course. He had to write checks to his suppliers, which took the bulk of a station's gross income. Farris paid distributors a couple of times a month and sometimes stretched the payments so that he only made one payment in a month. That meant he might have up to $100,000 sitting in his bank account. Lind earned interest while it was sitting there and was able to write checks on the money that wasn't technically his. As long as he kept bringing in cash to cover expenditures, he was fine. For the most part, he kept track of this in his head, though someone always made sure the books were balanced.

Because he was so canny about float, Lind often used it to his advantage. It helped him open new stations without incurring debt though he would sometimes ruffle the feathers of a distributor by being a few days late with a payment. Late, maybe, but he always paid. The distributors were making a lot of money off of his operations, so they let it slide.

CHAPTER SIX

SIGNS OF THE TIMES

Burma Shave pioneered humorous roadside signs in America. The brushless shaving cream company was well-known for its series of signs such as Does your husband / Misbehave / Grunt and grumble / Rant and rave / Shoot the brute some / Burma-Shave.

Lind admired the appeal of those signs, combining humor and advertising. A 1946 rabbit drive inspired the first humorous Stinker Station sign. Farmers and ranchers were reacting to a dramatic increase in jackrabbit populations by forming lines of men to walk through the sagebrush, scaring up rabbits, and shooting them. Lind put up a sign in the desert on the highway between Boise and Mountain Home that said, "Notice: Running Rabbits Have Right of Way!"

Years later, Lind told the story of the signs this way: "On one side we put a straight message—our gas. On the other, we'd put some squirrely [sic] thing like 'running rabbits have the right of way,' or 'It's uncanny, no rest rooms this area.' [People] soon learned there was something on each side of the sign... so here's the old Hollywood double-take—to see what's there and of course, the highways were only forty feet wide then" (Flanders, Farris 'Skunks' Competitors; Sells More Gas, 1976).

The two-sided signs came about almost by accident. As Lind explained in a 1969 Associated Press article, he bought a supply of interior grade plywood to make some of the first signs. It was all he could get at the time. "The plywood had to be painted on both sides to seal the sign against the moisture. As long as the back of the sign was painted, I got the idea of putting humor or curiosity-catching remarks on the back side" (Leeright, Gasoline Retailer Builds Booming Business on Humorous Ads, 1969).

In the 40s, 50s, and early part of the 60s, the federal government allowed signs to be put alongside highway rights-of-way on federal land. In southern Idaho, that land was usually sagebrush-covered, bleak, and boring to travel through.

The funny signs were a welcome break from the monotonous scenery.

Tourism promoters would likely point out that there is much to see in southern Idaho, and they would be correct. However, few of the best attractions in that part of the state are right alongside the major roads.

It is likely that another sign Lind put up would give promoters of tourism apoplexy today. It read, "Californians Entering Idaho Must Be Dipped!" Did you think a certain antipathy toward Californians coming to Idaho was a recent thing?

The governor of California sent Lind a letter asking him to remove the sign. Eventually, he did. It wasn't lost on him though, that the Stinker Station signs were getting publicity beyond the borders of Idaho.

Roadside signs had been a part of the promotional mix for Lind ever since that first station he managed in Twin Falls in 1936. He had used them since the beginning of the stations.

Uncanny Signs—The first Stinker Station sign read, "Notice: Running Rabbits Have Right of Way!" It was topical, if not memorable. There was a rabbit drive taking place when it went up. There are about a half dozen, including the one above, that people remember most often.

Skunky Signs—Several of the humorous signs tied in with the Stinker Station logo. So much so that one tourist stopped to ask about the "state skunk" she'd been seeing all across southern Idaho.

The new, humorous signs became important enough that by the early 1950s Lind set up sign painter Gus Roos in a sign shop behind the Orchard Street Stinker Station. Those plywood signs became metal.

Quoted in the Lind family book, Gus Roos said, "I was the one that did the large, ten-foot-high, two-sided skunk signs that Farris had me erect at his stations across Idaho and into Utah. I would lay out panels of sheet metal on a long table and paint sections of the skunk on the metal. Then using a truck that Farris had bought, I would load the panels onto it and drive them to the new station site where I would erect them atop a five-inch-wide steel post that was anchored in two feet of concrete. Sometimes Farris would assign a couple of fellows to assist me, or my son helped me on those assignments. Anyway, I erected signs for all his new stations, and I kept up the brightness by periodically touching up the color. It took roughly two weeks to paint, letter, and erect those signs" (Family, circa 2005, p. 145).

Perhaps Lind's most famous sign was erected near Bliss. In a field of lava rocks tumbled and smoothed by the Bonneville Flood, Roos planted a sign that said, "Petrified Watermelons—Take One Home to Your Mother-In-Law!" Roos painted a few rocks green to complete the effect.

People stopped and picked up rocks for souvenirs, some of them weighing as much as a hundred pounds. Roos went back more than once to paint up more rocks. They kept running out, so Lind trucked some in from another location, more than once (Crump, 2002).

A man named Harold E. Malde also stopped to look at the rocks. He happened to be a geologist. Malde was so intrigued by the sign, the rocks, and the petrified watermelons, that he mentioned it in Geological Survey Professional Paper 596. The scientific paper is about the impact of the Bonneville Flood. In it, he said, "In 1955, amused by a whimsical billboard that advertised one patch of boulders as 'petrified watermelons,' we applied to them the descriptive geological name Melon

Petrified Watermelons—This is easily the Stinker Station Sign most often remembered. Almost all the signs have been gone for years, but this one still exists on private property on Highway 30 near Bliss. The sign inspired the now common geological name for small boulders tumbled smooth by the prehistoric Bonneville Flood: Melon gravel.

A Little Risqué—Some signs tap danced up to the edge of offending polite company. Well, maybe not up to the edge, but you could see the edge from there. Mild as they were a few signs generated some objections, such as "Salt Lake City is Full of Lonely, Beautiful Women." That Utah sign was altered by taking out the word "lonely" to quiet complaints. A similar sign about Boise women raised not a peep.

Gravel, which has since become one of the many evocative terms in stratigraphic nomenclature" (Malde and Poweres, 1962, p. 1216).

So, how did Farris come up with all those sign sayings? He was a funny guy and created many of them himself. He also asked his family for help. Farris had a standing offer to pay 50 cents to anyone in the family who came up with a good line or two for the signs.

At one point, there were 150 signs between Green River, Wyoming, and Jordan Valley, Oregon. There were signs—and stations—in Utah and Nevada. An odd restriction on the Nevada signs perturbed Lind. Nevada law prohibited the use of the word "free" on outdoor advertising. "How are you going to advertise free ice if you can't use the word 'free,'" Lind wondered (Leeright, 1969).

It was in Utah where the signs caused a few complaints. One said, "Salt Lake City is Full of Lonely, Beautiful Women." He got enough complaints about that one, including a letter that called it obscene, that Lind had the word "lonely" deleted. A similar sign near Glenns Ferry referencing lonely Idaho women did not cause the same stir.

The Deseret News in the March 14, 1953 edition ran a story about Lind. They quoted him as saying, "I'll do anything for a laugh—and for a few dollars, I'll get hysterical."

That petrified watermelon sign was so popular it was moved from federal land to private property after the Highway Beautification Act of 1965 (see chapter 8), and it can still be seen near Bliss. The sign moved, and so did the highway. You get off I-84 and travel on US 30 to see it. The sign "WARNING TO TOURISTS—DO NOT LAUGH AT THE NATIVES" can be found on the Yellowstone Highway (US 26), mile marker 132 near Beachs Corner on the outskirts of Idaho Falls. Don't forget to stop and buy gas at the nearby Stinker Station.

Farris tried selling cars at one of his Boise stations. He had a Jaguar and MG franchise for

Laugh at Yourself—Lind's signs often poked fun at the reader. "Do You Have Rocks in Your Head? Get Refills Here," said one. Some, such as "Californians Must Be Dipped Before Entering Idaho" generated some complaints. It was the governor of California who took notice of that one.

Signing Off—At their peak about 150 Stinker Station signs were scattered around Utah, Wyoming, and Nevada, with the bulk of them being in southern Idaho. Most of them went away in the late 60s because of the Highway Beautification Act. The sign above is one of two that still exist. It is located near Beachs Corner in Idaho Falls on property owned by the company.

about a year. He had a little fun with it, but it didn't work out as a business, perhaps because the cars were too exotic for Boise at the time.

Lind tried other businesses in the automotive field. He tried selling tires at his gas stations and even opened a dedicated tire store. Selling tires at the stations turned out to be more trouble than it was worth because of the need to mount and balance the tires, which required shop space. The tire store didn't seem to hold his interest, and it closed, too. He built at least one restaurant and ran some bulk petroleum plants.

CHAPTER SEVEN

TRAGEDY

Farris Lind, who often relied on gut instinct in running his business and living his life, had a premonition in 1963. The first was when he was driving his family to get an oral vaccine that was believed to prevent polio. On that March day, he experienced an increasing feeling of dread. He was 47, long past the age when polio most often struck. He told himself he didn't really need to take the sugar cube. At the same time, he didn't want his family to miss out on the protection. Maybe he could palm the cube and just throw it away.

As he stood in line, watching others pay their 25 cents to get a tiny paper cup with a sugar cube inside, the feeling of dread intensified. Lind, quoted in the Lind family book, said, "I stood watching them and felt that I should not refrain, even though in my head there were lights flashing, bells ringing, and a feeling of dread or even cowardice."

When it was Lind's turn, he stepped forward, and a nurse handed him a paper cup. Lind said, "Well, here I go down into the Valley of the

Shadow." The nurse told him not to be so dramatic. He tipped the cube into his mouth.

In 1963, there were two types of polio vaccine. The Salk vaccine, created by Jonas Salk, was put into wide use in 1955. The Sabin Vaccine, created by Albert Sabin, was used commercially beginning in 1961. The Salk vaccine used inactivated poliovirus. It was an injection of essentially a dead virus. The Sabin vaccine used a weakened, but alive, poliovirus. It was administered orally by putting a drop on a sugar cube. Together, the two vaccines have eliminated polio from most of the world.

According to Vincent Racaniello, Ph.D., between 1961 and 1989 there was about one case of vaccine-associated paralytic poliomyelitis in the United States for every 2.9 million doses (Vincent Racaniello, 2015). Farris Lind would remain convinced for the rest of his life that he was one of those rare cases.

Within two days of taking the Sabin vaccine,

Farris was showing signs of paralysis. Days later he would be inside an iron lung, no longer able to breathe on his own. "I stood in line and paid my 25 cents to take the vaccine and was one of those unfortunate ones that contracted polio as a result. Within a few days after taking the vaccine, I had signs of paralysis and then lost the use of both arms and legs" (Leewright, 1969).

The two days between ingestion of the vaccine and the first indication he had polio would become crucial years later when Lind sued Wyeth Laboratories, the maker of the vaccine, in federal court. Lawyers for the defense argued that it was too soon for him to have contracted the disease from the sugar cube dose of weakened poliovirus. They said it was likely he had been infected during a trip to Mexico a week or two earlier.

The $3.5 million lawsuit went to a jury in 1970. In December of that year, at the close of testimony, the jury took four hours and 32 minutes to come back with a verdict. The Boise jurors decided that Lind had not contracted polio from the vaccine.

Farris Lind would never agree with that jury verdict. The strong premonition he had before taking the oral vaccine was proof enough for him.

CHAPTER EIGHT

FIGHTING THE FIRST LADY

In the years after he became paralyzed, Farris Lind was always looking for something to keep his mind busy. The lawsuit against Wyeth took some of his mind's energy, but it did not occupy his every waking thought. He had built his business on humor. Suddenly, in 1965 someone wanted to throw a bucket of cold water all over the most visible part of his funny business. That someone was Claudia Alta Johnson, better known as First Lady "Ladybird" Johnson.

The Highway Beautification Act (HBA) of 1965 was Ladybird Johnson's signature issue. She and her supporters were getting tired of the proliferation of billboards alongside federal highways in the United States. The act prohibited most outdoor advertising along Interstate and federal highways and required removal or screening of junkyards in highway viewsheds.

The law threatened a key component of Farris Lind's success. In 1969, he sued the State of Idaho because the Legislature had passed laws to bring the state into compliance with the HBA. Signs were not allowed within 660 feet of a federal highway right-of-way. Lind said, "The federal and state government have no right to deprive a farmer or other landowner of any rental income he can get from signs on his property. I owe it to myself to take a swing at bureaucracy" (Leeright, Stinker Battles Ad Law, 1969).

For signs on private property, Lind was paying $10-$15 a month rental. Some signs were on property he'd purchased.

The lawsuit asked that the highway beautification law be declared unconstitutional. Lind contended that it was unconstitutional because it prohibited the right to conduct a lawful business and impaired contractual arrangements Lind had with landowners.

The suit didn't gain any traction, and most of the signs came down, ending a run of about 25 years of memorable advertising.

CHAPTER NINE

CARRY ON

Lind would eventually regain partial use of his left hand, and he could move his head around a little. He would live the rest of his life dependent on various machines to help him breathe. That might have meant confinement to bed for someone else, but Lind took on the challenge the disease gave him by redoubling his efforts as a businessman. He could do much of that from his bed, but he wanted to see how his stations were operating. Farris bought a series of full-size convertibles to take him around. It was easier to load him and his equipment in a drop-top car. He eventually bought a motorhome to travel in.

In one sense, his illness gave him an advantage. He wanted to distract himself from the constant pain associated with his condition. Focusing on business was one way to do that. "As long as I'm confined to this bed with nothing to divert me from thinking and planning, I can out-think any man up and running around" (Family, Fearless Farris: the Incredible life of a courageous man, Circa 2005, p. 210).

A Nimble Mind—Farris Lind would never walk again after being struck by polio in 1963. He could move his head a little and eventually regained some movement in his left hand. His mind never stopped moving. He once said, "I can out-think any man up and running around."

National Recognition—Singer Pearl Bailey was the emcee in 1973 during the ceremony where Farris Lind was named Handicapped American of the Year. She concluded her remarks by saying, "Farris Lind, your home State of Idaho is proud of you as a very special son. We here today salute you as a valiant brother. And your Country is honored to call you Handicapped American of the Year."

For eight years, Lind continued to run his string of stations. By 1971 he had 25 fully owned Stinker Stations and another 15 where he was in partnership with someone else. He was Idaho's largest independent gasoline dealer. By that time, he had a lot of admirers, including Congressman Orval Hansen, who nominated him Handicapped American of the Year. President Richard Nixon awarded him that honor in 1973.

Singer Pearl Bailey emceed the program celebrating Lind's achievements. She said, "The years since 1963 [when Lind was stricken] must have been incredible ones. We can only guess at the initial shock, pain and despair. But we know they were years full of a family's love and devotion, of unceasing medical efforts to restore a helpless body. And most of all, they were years in which Farris Lind's faith and courage were equal to the test" (Extensions of Remarks, 1973).

The recognition that came with the national award started a new round of newspaper stories about Lind. Over the years, papers all across the country as well as in Canada and Great Britain had done stories about the Stinker Station signs. Now, though the signs got some attention, the man behind them was in the spotlight.

Shortly after Farris received the national honor in the White House, the *Idaho Statesman* featured him in a story by Steve Guerber on June 12, 1973. Lind explained that he could breathe for about ten minutes by gasping with his neck muscles, otherwise he depended on a respirator. "I think that's a pretty good life expectancy," Farris said, "Ten minutes without a battery" (Guy Goodine, 1971).

"I have a tracheotomy and the respirator blows air into my lungs and then, through a special valve, the air is sucked out—so the equipment does the breathing for me."

Lind believed "the live virus teamed up with some other unknown condition and created very serious problems."

The *Statesman* article stressed that Lind didn't

Distinguished Citizen—Lind was given many honors over the years, including the Idaho Statesman's *Distinguished Citizen Award, which included a portrait by John Collias (above). The recognition he enjoyed most was when that same paper ran the headline "Farris 'Skunks' Competitors; Sells More Gas." He had become Idaho's largest petroleum dealer, in spite of his paralysis, by using his mind.*

feel sorry for himself because of his condition. "I try to pretend there's nothing wrong with me and I try to do things I did before." He could type with a stick in his mouth. He hadn't learned to type before but found it a handy way to communicate. He conducted much of his business by telephone, keeping in touch with the office several times a day. Lind said he didn't feel handicapped as long as he had a head and a tongue he could use (Guerber, 1973).

His family had a lot of adjustments to make. Ginny Lind became his hands. Lind had always been a strong father. Now that was a challenge. He said, "It can be pretty difficult when the invalid father can't necessarily crack the whip sometimes because he's pinned to a mattress."

Lind carried on. He dealt with suppliers, handled publicity, created ads, and made the major decisions regarding his stations. He even expanded his personal fleet of trucks into a hundred rig commercial fleet, all from his chair and his bed.

"You have to fatigue the brain if you can't fatigue the body," Lind once said (Miller, 1976).

Lind kept that brain working all the time. It was a special moment for him in 1976 when the headline in the *Idaho Statesman* read, "Farris 'Skunks' Competitors; Sells More Gas." The $30 million corporation, with 28 stations in five states, was the number one petroleum retailer in Idaho.

"To be number one in peddling gas through brainpower and nimble footwork is probably more meaningful [than the national handicap award]. Though that was an achievement, it was a dubious one given just because your body is beat to hell, and you're playing a game where you ignore it. I would much prefer not to be eligible" (Flanders, 1976).

Fearless Farris was a tough businessman before polio struck. That didn't change when he became bedridden. Representatives from the Teamsters Union tried to bully Lind into giving union drivers some concessions he wasn't ready to give. He told them he'd rather sell his trucks and get out of the business. They called his bluff. The trucks went on the auction block and the drivers were out of their jobs.

Legacy—Farris Lind gave back to the community in many ways throughout his life. One particular passion of his was scouting. The family of Farris Lind worked with the Ore-Ida Council BSA to create the Farris C. Lind Scout Service Center in his honor. The center, located at 8901 W. Franklin Road in Boise, was dedicated on May 13, 1995. A sculpture of Farris Lind graces the lobby.

CHAPTER TEN

TRANSITIONS

Farris Lind was at the helm of his company until 1983 when he passed away at 67. His sons, Scott and Kent, had worked for the company for many years, and they were well-prepared to take over. They ran the Stinker Stations until 2002 when they decided it was time to retire. After more than 60 years operating under the leadership of Lind family members, long-time Stinker employee Shawn Davis and his business partner Charley Jones purchased the company. By that time the Stinker Stations included Arrowrock Supply, a grocery and tobacco wholesale company, and Westpoint Transportation, a fuel delivery company.

In 2011, Stinker acquired 14 additional convenience stores in Idaho when Albertsons decided to divest itself from the fuel business.

In 2012, Davis sold his share of the company to Charley Jones who continues to run it today.

Stinker Stores can be found all across Idaho, in Wyoming, and in Colorado. More than 900 people work for the company at 106 locations, 65 in Idaho. The business has come a long way since Farris Lind operated that cut-rate gas station in Twin Falls during the Great Depression, and since he opened his own station in Boise just before World War II. Today, Stinker Stores sell groceries and snack items, along with fuel, representing mainly Sinclair Oil.

Charley Jones was named Idaho Business Leader of 2011. The honor is given annually by the Delta Upsilon Chapter of Alpha Kappa Psi, a professional business fraternity at Idaho State University. Upon receiving the award, Jones said, "Business is an honorable profession, and the brightest and the best should consider it. Life is a journey, and where you are headed is more important than where you are. Re-invent, persevere and never quit. It's when you give up that you are truly defeated."

Stinker Station founder Farris Lind had a similar view on life and business. He would likely be proud of the company he started and of the team that runs it today.

CHAPTER ELEVEN

SUNDRY SIGNS, ETC.

THE FAIRLY DEFINITIVE LIST OF STINKER STATION SIGNS

AIN'T THIS MONOTONOUS?

ANY STRANGE TRACK FOUND IN THIS AREA BELONGS TO THE UNION PACIFIC

ARE YOU CRAZY ABOUT IDAHO? WE HAVE ALL SIZES OF STRAIGHT JACKETS

BE A THINKER--SEE THE STINKER

BEWARE OF CURVES AND SOFT SHOULDERS

Salt Lake City Station—The Stinker Stations started out a little slapdash. It wasn't long before Farris Lind upgraded them considerably. When he opened his flagship station in Salt Lake City in 1953, he called it "the Taj Mahal of service stations." It was the largest in Utah, costing $60,000, and featuring five islands with three pumps each. The rest rooms were finished in ceramic tile, and the location had a little something for fish. A fish pond with a running stream was a landscape feature of the station. (Photo courtesy of the Utah State Historical Society)

BEWARE--IDAHO IS FULL
OF LONELY BEAUTIFUL
WOMEN

CALIFORNIANS MUST
BE DIPPED BEFORE
ENTERING IDAHO

CATTLE COUNTRY--WATCH
OUT FOR BUM STEERS

DO NOT FEED DESERT
RATS

DO YOU HAVE A
RESERVATION, OR AREN'T
YOU AN INDIAN?

DO YOU HAVE ROCKS IN
YOUR HEAD? GET REFILLS
HERE

DO YOU SMELL
SOMETHING AWFUL? SO
DO WE!

DOES YOUR PAROLE
BOARD KNOW YOU'RE
HERE?

Some Skunks—Over the years the Stinker Station mascot had a lot of different looks depending who was drawing the skunk. It became more standardized and recognizable when it became the company's logo. Stepping out of my neutral author role for a moment, I admit the skunks used to drive me crazy. Most of them had the strips on the front. As an Idaho farm boy I knew that was just not right. Over the years I came to realize the necessity of the front-mounted stripes. Without them, the mascot could be mistaken for a cat. We wouldn't want that, would we?

DON'T JUST SIT THERE--
NAG YOUR HUSBAND

DON'T WASH YOUR
BRITCHES IN FARMER'S
DITCHES

DRIVE AT NIGHT--THERE'S
MORE MOONSHINE THEN

DRIVE CAREFULLY--
THERE'S NO FUTURE IN
SUICIDE

DURING RAINY SEASON
WATCH OUT FOR
COWSLIPS AND BULRUSHES

FARM GIRLS ARE NOT
PRAIRIE CHICKENS OR
DRY FARM TOMATOES

FISHERMEN BEWARE OF
LOAN SHARKS

FISHERMEN--DO YOU HAVE
WORMS?

Sporty Skunks—In 1949 you could pick up a skiing skunk decal at the Stinker Stations. Today, at the Stinker Stores, you're likely to see an updated skunk skiing, or even snowboarding.

FOR A FAST PICKUP PASS
A STATE PATROLMAN

GET YOUR RADIOACTIVE
RATTLESNAKES AT
FAGAN'S PET SHOP

GRIZZLY BEAR FEEDING
GROUNDS. COUNT YOUR
CHILDREN, WATCH YOUR
HONEY

HAVE TEA WITH ME--
BRING YOUR OWN BAG

HISTERICAL MARKER-
-CHIEF SACATABACA
STARVED TO DEATH HERE

HISTERICAL MARKER-
-WASHINGTON SLEPT
HERE* *SO DID OREGON

IDAHO'S SKUNKS ARE NOT
TO BE SNIFFED AT

IDAHO'S STRONGEST
ANIMAL--THE SKUNK

Skunkity Skunk Skunk—In the photo above from 1953, Farris Lind himself seems a little skeptical of something called Skunk Oil. He did not hesitate to put the fighting skunk on items ranging from window stickers to window scrapers. (Photo courtesy of the Utah State Historical Society)

IF YOU LIVED HERE YOUD
BE HOME NOW (SPELLING
MISTAKE)

IF YOUR WIFE WANTS TO
DRIVE, DON'T STAND IN
HER WAY

INDIANS MUST NOT SCALP
TOURISTS WITHIN 300
FEET OF HIGHWAY

IS YOUR CLUTCH
SLIPPING? LET US CHECK
YOUR REAR END

IT'S LUCKY YOU HAVE
FRIENDS OR YOU'DE
BE A TOTAL STRANGER
(SPELLING ERROR)

IT'S UNCANNY--NO REST
ROOMS IN THIS AREA

LET THERE BE A MINUTE
OF SILENCE WHILE WE
CHANGE BACK SEAT
DRIVERS

Stinker Soap—Fearless Farris was always on the lookout for something he could slap a skunk on. These bars of soap were a popular item, probably not so much for their cleaning ability as for their skunkiness. (Photos from the collection of Aaron Esparza)

LET US CHECK YOUR
BAGGAGE FOR STOLEN
TOWELS

LONELY HEARTS CLUB
PICNIC AREA

LOST? KEEP GOING--YOU
ARE MAKING GOOD TIME
ANYWAY

NEXT TIME TAKE
THE COOL ROUTE GO
UNDERGROUND

NO FISHING WITHIN 100
YARDS OF THE ROAD

NO FISHING--SUCKERS

NO HUNTING DOGS IN
THIS AREA--YOU CAN'T
FIND ONE ANYWAY

NO TRESSPASSING--THIS
AREA IS FOR THE BIRDS

NUDE SWIMMING
PROHIBITED IN THIS AREA

So Special—Kitsch is a German word that often refers to popular art as opposed to highbrow art. Kitsch, or kitschy, is synonymous with tacky. Often, it's so bad, or just plain silly, that people collect it for just that reason. These salt and pepper shakers could themselves be the dictionary definition. Note that this pair of Stinkers was manufactured in Japan, back when that meant cheap. (Photo from the collection of Aaron Esparza)

NUDIST AREA--KEEP EYES ON ROAD--COWBOYS PLEASE REMOVE SPURS

NUDISTS TRY OUR BEAR GREASE FOR THAT SLICK LOOK

OUR GAS CONTAINS LANOLIN--IT KEEPS YOUR PISTONS SOFT AND LOVELY

PETRIFIED FOREST--UNIONIZED WOODPECKERS KEEP OUT

PETRIFIED WATERMELONS--TAKE ONE HOME TO YOUR MOTHER-IN-LAW

PRISON AREA--DO NOT PICK UP HITCHIKERS

QUIET PLEASE--ENTERING GHOST TOWN

Sizzling Skunk—About 75 percent of the original Stinker Station at 16th and Front in Boise was destroyed by fire in the early morning of December 22, 1950. Always on the lookout for opportunity, Farris Lind used the fire as a good excuse for an attention-getting ad.

QUIET PLEASE--HOOT
OWLS ARE SLEEPING

RAIN CHECKS CASHED,
SUCKERS WELCOME--
BANK OF SNAKE RIVER

RATTLESHAKE PICNIC
GROUNDS--TOURISTS
WELCOME

READ TO RESTLESS KIDS
(THE RIOT ACT)

REPORT INDIAN
MASSACRES TO YOUR
DOCTOR

REPORT SMOKE SIGNALS
TO WESTERN UNION (10
WESTERN COUNTIES)

REPORT SNAKES TO YOUR
DOCTOR

RUNNING RABBITS HAVE
RIGHT OF WAY

Skunks on His Mind—Several themes showed up on the signs, back seat drivers, mothers-in-law, fake warnings. About a half dozen of the signs had that familiar whiff of skunk.

S* BOMB FALLOUT AREA--
*SKUNK

SAGE BRUSH IS FREE--
TAKE SOME HOME TO
YOUR MOTHER-IN-LAW

SAVE LIKE MAD--
FEARLESS FARRIS--
STINKER STATION

SHEEPHERDERS HEADED
FOR TOWN HAVE THE
RIGHT OF WAY

SITE OF DUST BOWL
GAME--FARMERS VS
GOPHERS

SITE OF POLECAT
MASSACRE--IDAHO'S
GREATEST POLITICAL
STINK

SITTING BULL STOOD UP
HERE

SKUNK CROSSING AHEAD--
CLOSE WINDOWS

Collectable—Yes, there are sign collectors out there. Old Stinker Station signs are highly collectible because of that skunk. He's a beauty in neon with that flashing tail. (Photo courtesy of John Bertram)

SMOKERS PUT OUT
YOUR BURNING BUTTS-
-REMEMBER, BUFFALO
CHIPS ARE FLAMMABLE

SOUND BARRIER BROKEN
HERE--WATCH OUT FOR
PIECES

STATE HIGHWAY
OBSTACLE COURSE

THE EYES OF TAXES ARE
UPON YOU

THE ONLY CORN RAISED
IN THE DESERT ARE THESE
SIGNS

THINK BIG--RAISE
ELEPHANTS

THIS AREA IS FOR
THE BIRDS--IT'S FOWL
TERRITORY

THIS IS NOT SAGE BRUSH!
YOU'RE IN IDAHO CLOVER

Misteaks—He made few. But then again, too few to mention. Almost. One wonders how many friends of Farris pointed out that "you'de" isn't an actual word.

THIS IS SHEEP COUNTRY--LET US PULL THE WOOL OVER YOUR EYES

THIS ROAD FOR WOMEN ONLY--MEN TAKE DETOUR--UNLESS ACCOMPANIED BY WIFE OR GUARDIAN

UNLAWFUL TO SPEAR SALMON OR SHOOT CRAPS IN THIS AREA

WANT A COOL MILLION? TAKE HOME A FROZEN ANTHILL

WARNING TO TOURISTS--DO NOT LAUGH AT THE NATIVES

WARNING--BOISE IS FULL OF TAXPAYERS

WARNING--DO NOT DISTURB BREEDING REACTORS (SKUNKS)

Raising a Stink on Orchard—The Orchard Street Stinker Station served as the headquarters of the company for a time. It was here, too, where Gus Roos turned out all those cheeky signs. This picture was taken circa 1960. (Photo courtesy of John Bertram)

WARNING--DO NOT FEED
OR DISTURB NESTING
COYOTES

WARNING--LIONS, MOOSE,
ELK, EAGLES PAY YOUR
DUES

WARNING--METHODISTS
WATCH OUT FOR MORMON
CRICKETS

WARNING--THE WIND WILL
BLOW THIS ROAD

WATCH FOR SNOWSLIDES
AND SUNDOGS

WEEKEND DRIVERS,
USE OUR PRICKLY PEAR
CUSHIONS--GIVES YOU A
LIFT

WELCOME TO POTOMAC-
-SLOW DOWN--THIS IS A
ONE HEARSE TOWN

WELCOME TO UGLY MEN
AND BEAUTIFUL WOMEN

Grizzly Country—It looks "bearly" possible that you might run into a grizzly here. Notice how thick the sagebrush and rabbit brush was. Decades of wildfire have made the desert scenery in Idaho quite a lot different today.

WHAT'S EATING YOU?
THE NATIVES ARE NOT
CANNIBALS

WHY BE A WAGE SLAVE?
FIND YOUR WIFE A JOB

WHY BE DISAGREEABLE?
WITH A LITTLE EFFORT
YOU CAN BE A STINKER

WHY GO TO SIBERIA?
WORK IN OUR SALT MINES

WITH A LATER START YOU
WOULDN'T BE HERE YET

WRITE TO YOUR PEN
PALS--THE PAROLE BOARD

Still There—Perhaps the most famous Stinker Station sign is now on private property and off the beaten path where it is seldom seen. You'll find it less than two miles south of the King Hill exit, Exit 129, off I-84 on Old Highway 30. It's on the right at the intersection with 101 Ranch Road.

Horses?...NO!
Man's Best Friend Is a SKUNK!

Horses pulled a few wagons but the STINKER has pushed more cars farther and faster than any stallion in Idaho.

HE'S THE WORLD'S STRONGEST SKUNK

In fact, this skunk has raised quite a stink. From New York to California, the smell has reached the "Big Boys" in plush offices. They don't like the scent of this Stinker's low prices. So, the Squeeze Play is on. They've passed the word down to lower prices and subsidize their dealers. They want to punish the Stinker —but he's fighting back... he's STILL UNDERSELLING all the Big Boys. Keep Gas Prices down. BUY FROM THE GUY WHO BROKE THE PRICE...your Local Independent Idaho Stinker. Regardless of price—regardless of brand—YOU CAN'T BUY A BETTER GAS...ANYWHERE!

The Squeeze Play Is On... But The STINKER FIGHTS BACK

BUY CUT-RATE GAS
from
Fearless Farris

1620 Front Street, Boise
Opposite High School, Nampa

FREE COMIC BOOKS
Children Accompanied by Their Parents Will Be Given a Comic Book Free.

FREE! STINKER STICKERS *In Color*

Get Yours NOW!
IDAHO'S WESTERN* BADMAN SKUNK
• New • Novel • Colorful

For Your Windshield to Identify a Thinking Motorist and Idaho Booster!

An attractive windshield decal in color of the STINKER in western garb and pants, too — ABSOLUTELY FREE — drive into Idaho's finest service station, the envy of the big boys, for yours today.

This decal is the badge of a thrifty motorist who is used to the best—UNSURPASSED QUALITY, and is wise enuff to save money on every king-sized gallon of STINKER guaranteed gasoline. This emblem also seems to act as a good-luck charm and is credited with keeping away traffic cops, mumps, flat tires and hangovers. Some game wardens accept a STINKER STICKER instead of a fishing license and progressive bankers prefer them to a chattel mortgage. Even employes of big competitive companies often carry them hidden in their billfolds, waiting for the day when they hand one to the boss as a combined resignation and unbearable insult avengeable only in blood. Iron Curtain Countries and Monopolies recognize this decal as a secret weapon that raises the downtrodden and brings forth free enterprise.

* Meaner and Smellier than Eastern Skunks.

Fearless Farris
STINKER STATIONS
16th and Front - Boise Across from the High School - Nampa

Every Morning When I Get Up,

I HATE MYSELF

because

I SELL GAS...

The Stinker

FOR LESS [The World's Best Gas For Less]

... Fearless Farris sells top-quality *Gasoline* at *Cut Rate Prices* to his friends and has not an enemy in the entire Boise Valley.

... Eight years of fair dealing with his friends has caused the people of this valley to place dependence in "the stinker," his products, and his service.

Fearless Farris Stands for

Top Quality Gas at Cut Rates

the speediest service in Boise... and SATISFACTION to everyone.

Fearless Farris

1620 FRONT ST.

"At the Sign of the Skunk"

A Good Sign—Lady Bird Johnson's campaign to get rid of signs along federal highways all but killed Farris Lind's best marketing gimmick. If the Stinker Station signs were the only ones out there cluttering up the scenery, few would object. America's roadways were plastered with billboards, though. In this shot there are at least five other signs in the background clamoring for the attention of drivers. Good riddance to most of them. A fond farewell to the skunks.

WORKS CITED

Crump, S. (2002, May 26). To Fearless Farris, Idaho's Poet of Empty. *Twin Falls Times News*.

Extensions of Remarks. (1973, May 7). Congressional Record . Washington, DC: U.S. Congress.

Family, L. (Circa 2005). Fearless Farris: the Incredible life of a Courageous man. J.B. Media International.

Farris Lind... Flotsam on a Gasoline Sea. (1959, May 31). *Salt Lake Tribune*, p. 16.

Flanders, P. (1976, May 6B). Farris 'Skunks' Competetitors; Sells More Gas. *Idaho Statesman*.

Guerber, S. (1973, June 12). Stricken by Polio at 47, Boise Oil Dealer Adjusts, Prospers. *Idaho Statesman*.

Guy Goodine, U. (1971, July 4). Paralyzed Tulsa Man Runs His Own Business. *Tampa Tribune-Times*. (Note mistake in title)

Leeright, B. (1969, September 23). *Idaho State Journal*, pp. Section C, Page 1.

Leeright, B. (1969, November 24). Gasoline Retailer Builds Booming Business on Humorous Ads. *Idaho Statesman*, p. 29.

Leeright, B. (1969, December 12). Stinker Battles Ad Law. *Capital Journal*, p. 29.

Leeright, B. (1969, October 19). Owner of Stinker Stations Battles Idaho Curbs on Roadside Billboards. *Idaho Statesman*, p. 23.

Miller, A. (1976, July 5). Paralysis 'Barely Slows' Fearless. *Idaho Statesman*.

Vincent Racaniello, P. (2015). Why do we still use Sabin poliovirus vaccine? Retrieved from virology.ws: http://www.virology.ws/2015/09/10/why-do-we-still-use-sabin-poliovirus-vaccine/

Made in the USA
Thornton, CO
01/21/23 12:50:07

29bd2f27-8118-4cdf-85d2-e60415180dcdR01

This is the story of the signs, the skunk, the crop dusting, the tragedy and the triumph of a man who was the essence of Idaho.

Mr. Nash wrote,
I think that I shall never see
A billboard lovely as a tree...
yet had he only read Just's book,
surely he'd have added:
Out in the sage the Stinker signs
Amply served for the missing pines.

---Cort Conley, Author of *Idaho for the Curious*

With the inclusion of a wonderful collection of photographs and a well-researched list of these road-s sayings, writer/historian Just chronicles the inspiring story of Fearless Farris, bringing back memories many of us and introducing this iconic Idahoan to new and future generations.

--Kelly Jones, author of *Evel Knievel Jumps the Snake River Canyon and Other Stories Close to H*

Rick Just is a native Idahoan who grew up on a ranch along the Blackfoot River. He is the author of several books including *Keeping Private Idaho* and *The Kids Guide to Boise.* He writes a daily Idaho history blog on Facebook called Speaking of Idaho.